I DO THIS LEFT-HANDED.

Sky Pony Press books may be purchased in bulk at special discounts for sales promotion, corporate gifts, fund-raising, or educational purposes. Special editions can also be created to specifications. For details, contact the Special Sales Department, Sky Pony Press, 307 West 36th Street, 11th Floor, New York, NY 10018 or info@skyhorsepublishing.com.

Sky Pony® is a registered trademark of Skyhorse Publishing, Inc.®, a Delaware corporation.

Visit our website at www.skyponypress.com.

10 9 8 7 6 5 4 3 2 1

Manufactured in China, August 2022
This product conforms to CPSIA 2008

Library of Congress Cataloging-in-Publication Data is available on file.

Cover design by Kai Texel
Cover illustrations by Dagmar Geisler
US Edition edited by Nicole Frail

Print ISBN: 978-1-5107-7097-3
Ebook ISBN: 978-1-5107-7099-7

I Am Left-Handed!

What I Love About Being a Lefty

Written by **Dagmar Geisler & Stephanie Gerharz**

Illustrated by **Dagmar Geisler**

Translated by **Andy Jones Berasaluce**

Sky Pony Press
New York

I do everything with my left hand.
That's because I'm left-handed.

That means I do a lot of things with my left hand. Like
eating or drawing or brushing my teeth. Most people do
all this with their right hands. But many people use their
left hands—more people than you might think!

Some examples of left-handed people are . . .

Albert Einstein

Picasso

Jimi Hendrix

My mama

Queen Elizabeth

My grandpa

Bart Simpson

Goethe

Lady Gaga

And . . .
And . . .
And . . .

Mr. Ömer from the farmers' market

Mozart and Beethoven

How do I know if I'm left-handed or right-handed?

Everyone has one side called your "strong" side.

You'll find out which side it is because that's the hand automatically reaching for an object.

Or the hand waving when your visitors are leaving.

Or the hand on top when you're clapping.
Try it now. Which hand isn't moving and
which one's doing the clapping?

Sometimes you can even see in your baby pictures
which hand's going to be the strong one.

It's all actually pretty easy.

This could be because people have always assumed that right-handed people are the majority. And since people previously thought that only one way could be correct, the world focused on right-handed people.

So unfair!

PRECISELY.

It starts with eating. Suppose we have tasty carrot soup. The table is set, and the spoons are all on the right side of the bowls.

Everyone picks theirs up and—**IN ONE SWOOP**— it seems I feel weird.

It's rather strange how seldom some people think about just how many lefties there are.

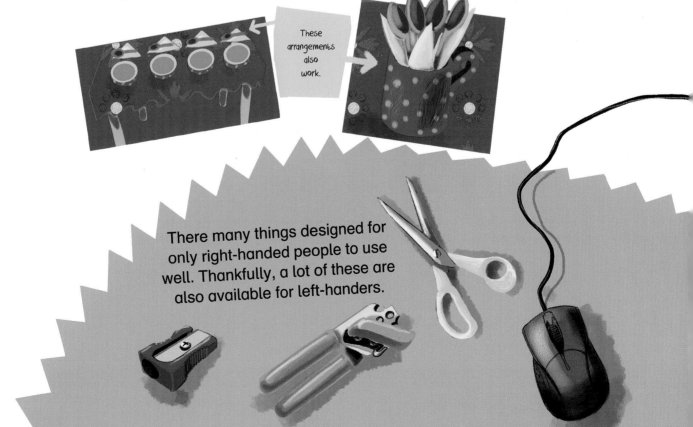

How is it then that some of us are left-handed and others right-handed?

It's something inherited, like your eye and hair color. It's in our genes.

That means whether your left or right side is your strong one is established before you come into the world. If left's your strong side, then you're left-handed.

Often, but not always, the same is true for your feet. Pay attention to which foot goes for the ball when playing soccer or which foot wants to take the first step when walking.

All this is controlled in your brain. When you want to grab an apple, the command comes from your brain.

THE BRAIN HAS TWO HEMISPHERES THAT ARE JOINED TOGETHER.

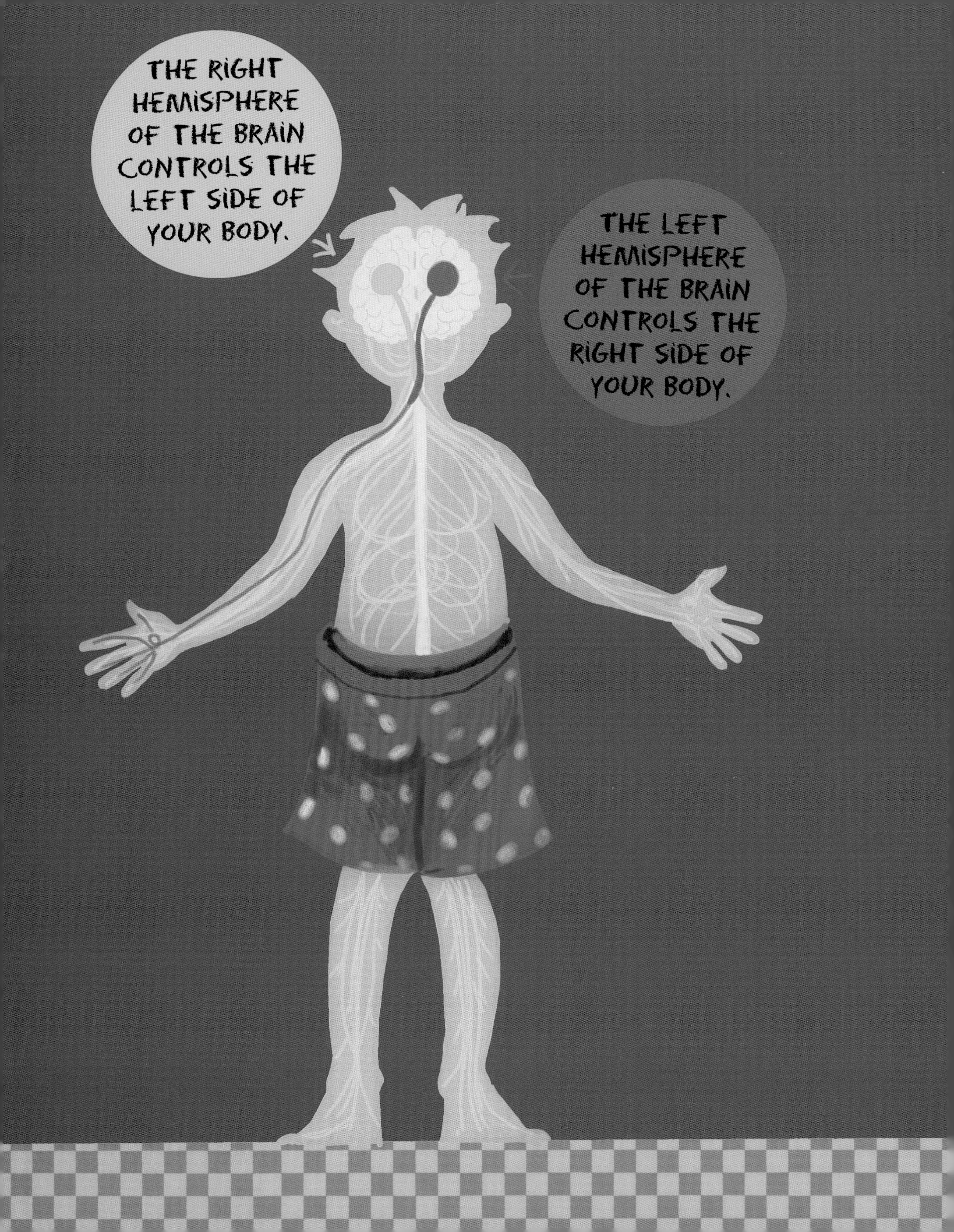
THE RIGHT HEMISPHERE OF THE BRAIN CONTROLS THE LEFT SIDE OF YOUR BODY.
THE LEFT HEMISPHERE OF THE BRAIN CONTROLS THE RIGHT SIDE OF YOUR BODY.

No, it doesn't mean that at all. Each side has its own strengths.

Everything we do turns out especially well when each side takes on what it does best.

FOR EXAMPLE:

When you want to cut something out, your strong hand holds the scissors.
If you're left-handed, there are scissors for lefties.
Your strong hand tries to cut precisely along the line while your eyes monitor it.
And what's the other hand doing?
It keeps turning and rotating the page in exactly the right direction—without you having to think about it.
This goes for peeling apples or carrots and cucumbers, too.
And with many other activities!

OUR TWO SIDES ARE A STRONG TEAM.

THAT MAKES A MESS IN YOUR HEAD.

That's what happened to Lukas. He's actually left-handed, but he didn't know that until recently and did everything with his right hand.

That was because the others in his family use their right hands. Lukas just imitated them.
It never occurred to him that he could use the other hand, too.

When all the kids started to write their names, this is how Lukas wrote his:

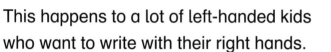

This happens to a lot of left-handed kids who want to write with their right hands.

They first write as if reflected in a mirror. And they prefer to start writing on the page's right side because it feels better.

Lukas didn't feel like writing more.

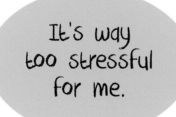

It's way too stressful for me.

Lukas's mom knew some people in their family were left-handed. Lukas's grandfather, who lives far away in northern Germany, is one. When his grandfather was a boy, he was punished for using his left hand. That's how it used to be!

Lukas's mom made an appointment for Lukas and herself with the handedness consultant (that's the name!).

Information
Center for Lefthanded People
Handedness Consultancy*

Lukas's mom even decided to get herself tested, too.

*This specific organization is based in Germany, where Lukas lives. In North America, you can make an appointment with an occupational therapist, or OT.

The consultant tested both of them. Lukas was very surprised by how much fun it was. The tests made it clear: Lukas is left-handed for sure— and his mom is, too!

"Well, would you look at that!" says Mom. She thought of the many times when she had felt a bit odd. When playing table tennis when she was younger, she wanted to take the paddle in her left hand, and everyone had told her she was wrong.

The counselor asked both of them if they wanted to do some retraining.

That means doing exercises so the left hand gets used to its role as the strong one.

Lukas absolutely wanted that, but his mother still had to think about it for herself.

The counselor then wanted to know if the rest of the family would also support Lukas with his training.

"Definitely!" Mom said.

LUKAS-MOBILE

FOR MAMA

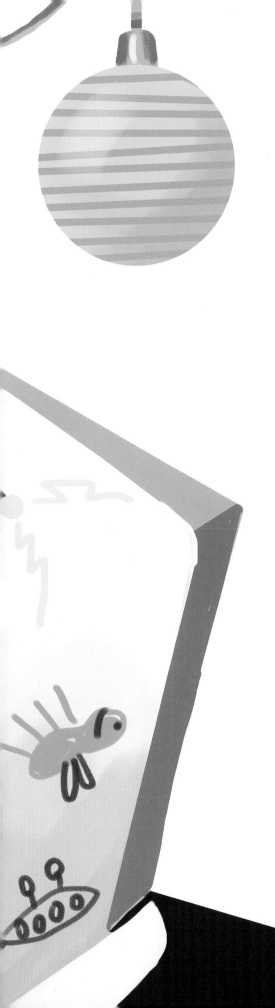

Lukas has been doing his exercises for a while now and keeps going back to counseling for left-handers.

At first, he had to take breaks more often, because it's quite a strenuous adjustment for the brain.

But now that he knows he can draw and write equally well with his left hand, he has a lot more fun.

Lukas's mom has noticed that he's no longer as fidgety and inattentive as he was.

"I'm in a much better mood, too. Did you notice?" asks Lukas.

TO WORK, YOU NEED TO HAVE GOOD LIGHT. FOR LEFT-HANDERS, IT'S BEST IF IT COMES FROM THE RIGHT. THEN THE HAND THAT WRITES DOESN'T CAST A SHADOW ON THE PAPER.

To make a space suitable for left-handed people to draw and write, here are a few tips and tricks:

I do everything left-handed

WHICH THE SIDE THE TREATS ARE ON DOESN'T MATTER.

IF SEVERAL KIDS ARE WORKING AT A TABLE, THE LEFT-HANDED KID SITS ON THE FAR LEFT, OR ELSE ELBOWS GET IN THE WAY. NATURALLY, THIS DOESN'T HAPPEN IF TWO LEFT-HANDERS SIT NEXT TO EACH OTHER.

SUCH DESK PADS CAN ALSO BE BOUGHT READY-MADE.

TO WRITE EASILY, IT'S IMPORTANT THAT THE PAPER LIE CORRECTLY. WITH A DESK PAD LIKE THIS, IT'S VERY SIMPLE TO FIND THE CORRECT POSITION. IT'S GOOD TO SIT UP STRAIGHT. WHEN WRITING, THE TOP OF THE PEN POINTS TOWARD THE LEFT SHOULDER.

We left-handers, just like right-handers, need things that work well for us.

To be able to write easily, there are certain desk pads.

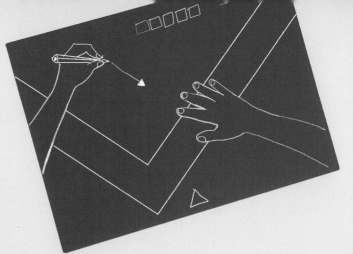

It's good to hold the pen/pencil using a three-finger grip.

There are pencils/pens that make this easy to do smoothly. It's handy to have pens with recessed grips or thick triangular pencils.

Using external grips also helps you hold other pens/pencils well.

Lefty scissors have the cutting edge on the other side, so we can see where we're cutting.

Left-handed rulers have the numbers the other way around. This makes it easier to draw lines.

With a pencil sharpener like this, I can turn the pencil around the right way.

WRITING PAD FOR LEFTIES

The rings on the writing pad are on the right so that they don't bother the left hand.

A soup ladle for left-handers is good because then the carrot soup lands in the bowl.

The vegetable peelers have a sharp blade on the right side.

And the most important of all is the lefty can opener!

There's even more worth knowing for us lefties. For example:

There are guitars, violins, flutes, and other musical instruments made special for us.

When a righty wants to show you something, just watch in the mirror. Then it's the correct way around for you.

Aha!

Left-handers are world champions at table tennis and other sports!

Left-handers tie their shoelaces the other way around.

On bikes, the bell and the grip for the stronger rear wheel brake go on the left.

Hmmmmm!

A few exercises help keep the two halves of your brain working well together. They create fresh energy when you feel a little groggy or can no longer concentrate as much.

You can dance while tapping your left hand to your right knee and your right hand to your left knee. Keep alternating. It's really fun when you play your favorite music at the same time. You can also tap your elbows to your knees.

With your strong hand, draw a horizontal figure eight in the air. To do this, stretch out your arm, start in the middle, and draw using sweeping motions. Then you do the same with the other hand.

The point where the lines cross should ideally be between your eyes.

Put your fingertips together in front of your stomach. Then breathe in and out deeply and imagine how the two hemispheres of your brain work together. Keep breathing and think of something nice.

That does you good.

Miss Mary Mack, Mack, Mack
All dressed in black, black, black

Certain clapping games refresh you and are fun. Which ones do you know? Ask your friends and relatives which clapping games they know. Then try them out together.

And what our brain also needs is enough water. Water conducts energy through our body so everything runs optimally.

WHEN BOTH OUR BRAIN'S HEMISPHERES ARE WELL CONNECTED, WE CAN SUCCEED AT ALMOST ANYTHING.

Resources

**First German Consultancy and Information Center
for Lefthanders and Converted Lefthanders**

www.lefthander-consulting.org
www.linkshaenderforum.org

You can find a great deal of information on both websites about books, information centers, German consultants for left-handers, and German stores for left-handers. But there's also some great information for English-speaking lefties here, too! You'll find all the valuable information about and for left-handers on this site.

You can also check out:

www.lefthandedchildren.org
www.leftyslefthanded.com
www.lefthanders.org
www.lefthandersday.com

Don't forget! Since 1976, August 13 has been International Left-Handers Day!

AFTERWORD

In this book, it becomes clear what it means to be left-handed in a right-handed-dominated and -oriented world.

This book should help create a deeper awareness of lefties, thus helping others become more sensitive to individualities. You can certainly count on an "aha!" moment or two.

A lot of this information is unfortunately not anchored in people's consciousness. That's why we want to help create more awareness with this book. We don't just want to inform, however—we also want to sharpen the focus on left-handed people and make their journeys, which aren't always easy, easier. This begins as early as infancy.

We feel the need to address children, in particular, and to present them with the child-friendly version of information otherwise intended only for adults. Dagmar Geisler implemented the content very expressively, with a lot of humor.

In closing, I'd like to emphasize one thing in particular: Everyone is welcome to read this work, including right-handed people!

Wishing you lots of fun,
Stephanie Gerharz

Dagmar Geisler has already supported several generations of parents in accompanying their children through emotionally difficult situations. With her Safe Child, Happy Parent picture book series, the author and illustrator sensitively deals with the most important issues related to growing up, from body awareness to the exploration of your own emotional world to social interaction.

Her works always include a helping of humor, especially so when the matter is serious.

Her books have been translated into twenty languages and have been published in the United States and elsewhere.

Stephanie Gerharz was born in London in 1965 and is the mother of two adult children. She worked in a child and adolescent psychiatric practice until she set up her own practice. There, she accompanies children and adults in their processes as a coach and left-hander consultant. As an author, she self-published the card set *Kopfsalat mit Herz*, a game to promote mindfulness and heart qualities.

I STILL DO THIS WITH MY LEFT HAND.

I DO THIS LEFTY.